Home Is Where the DÖG Is

Artwork by Brett Longley

HARVEST HOUSE PUBLISHERS

EUGENE, OREGON

Artwork © 2007 by Brett Longley and used by Harvest House Publishers, Inc., under authorization. For more information regarding art prints featured in this book, please contact Brett Longley at dogguy@mac.com

Design and production by Garborg Design Works, Savage, Minnesota

Harvest House Publishers has made every effort to trace the ownership of all poems and quotes. In the event of a question arising from the use of a poem or quote, we regret any error made and will be pleased to make the necessary correction in future editions of this book.

HOME IS WHERE THE DOG IS
Text copyright © 2007 by Harvest House Publishers
Published by Harvest House Publishers
Eugene, Oregon 97402

ISBN-13: 978-0-7369-1970-8
ISBN-10: 0-7369-1970-8

Printed in China

07 08 09 10 11 12 13 /LP/ 10 9 8 7 6 5 4 3 2 1

Paintings Featured in Book:

Cover	Sibling Rivalry
pg 3	Kindred
4	You've Got Peanut Butter on my Chocolate
5	Jet Lab
6	Bootleg
7	I'm Going Home
9	Keeper of the Hog
10	8 Inches and 10 Below
11	Windows
12	Walking the Dog
13	Triple A
15	Reflections
16	Smudge
17	Snow Fun Alone
19	Review
20	Ok I'm Going to Count to 10
22	Quack Attack
23	Engaged
24	Make Me
26	Gesundheit
27	a) Oh to Joe b) Life
31	Two for One
32	Quack Attack the Duck Strikes Back

In the late summer afternoon, when the teacups were cleared, and the family went inside...the dogs who are no longer under human command, find delight in the company of each other.

JOE DUNNEA

4

I think we are drawn to dogs because they are the uninhibited creatures we might be if we weren't certain we knew better.

GEORGE BIRD EVANS

Since he had started playing with his father's hound puppies a great dream had grown within him. Some day he would find a dog to shame all others, a fine dog that he could treasure, and cherish, and breed from so that all who loved fine dogs would come to see and buy his. That would be all he wanted of Heaven.

JIM KJELGAARD
Big Red

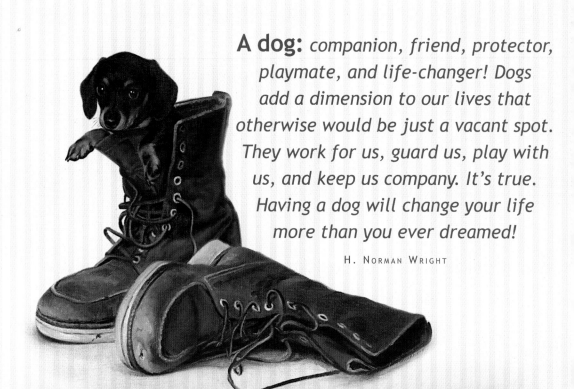

A dog: *companion, friend, protector, playmate, and life-changer! Dogs add a dimension to our lives that otherwise would be just a vacant spot. They work for us, guard us, play with us, and keep us company. It's true. Having a dog will change your life more than you ever dreamed!*

H. NORMAN WRIGHT

Money will buy you a pretty good dog, but it won't buy the wag of his tail.

HENRY WHEELER SHAW

If a picture wasn't going very
well I'd put a puppy dog in it,
always a mongrel, you know, never
one of the full-bred puppies.

NORMAN ROCKWELL

7

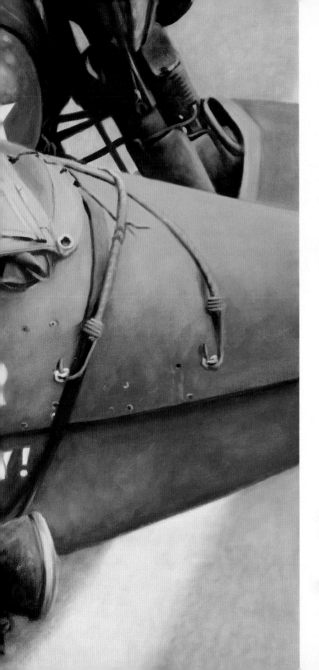

In order to really enjoy a dog,
one doesn't merely try to
train him to be semi-human.
The point of it is to open
oneself to the possibility of
becoming partly a dog.

EDWARD HOAGLAND

I like driving around
with my two dogs,
especially on the
freeways. I make
them wear little
hats so I can use the
car-pool lanes.

MONICA PIPER

The poor dog,
in life the firmest friend,
The first to welcome,
foremost to defend.

Dogs are our link to paradise. They don't know evil or jealousy or discontent. To sit with a dog on a hillside on a glorious afternoon is to be back in Eden, where doing nothing was not boring—it was peace.

The fact remains that he is there in our houses, as ancient, as rightly placed, as perfectly adapted to our habits as though he had appeared on this earth, such as he now is, at the same time as ourselves. We have not to gain his confidence or his friendship: he is born our friend; while his eyes are still closed, already he believes in us; even before his birth, he has given himself to man. But the word "friend" does not exactly depict his affectionate worship. He loves us and reveres us as though we had drawn him out of nothing. He is, before all, our creature full of gratitude, and more devoted than the apple of our eye.

The dog was created especially for children.

HENRY WARD BEECHER

In their sympathies, children feel nearer animals than adults. They frolic with animals, caress them, share with them feelings neither has words for. Have they ever stroked any adult with the love they bestow on a cat? Hugged any grownup with the ecstasy they feel when clasping a puppy?

JESSAMYN WEST

If you are going
to run away
from home, take
a dog along.

WILLIAM LEAST HEAT-MOON

13

To those who have cherished an affection for a faithful and
sagacious dog, I need hardly be at the trouble of explaining the
nature or the intensity of the gratification thus derivable. There is
something in the unselfish and self-sacrificing love of a brute, which
goes directly to the heart of him who has had frequent occasion to
test the paltry friendship and gossamer fidelity of mere Man.

EDGAR ALLAN POE
The Black Cat

By and large, people who enjoy teaching animals to roll over will find themselves happier with a dog.

BARBARA HOLLAND

To my way of thinking there's something wrong, or missing, with any person who hasn't got a soft spot in their heart for an animal of some kind. With most folks the dog stands highest as man's friend, then comes the horse, with others the cat is liked best as a pet, or a monkey is fussed over; but whatever kind of animal it is a person likes, it's all hunky dory so long as there's a place in the heart for one or a few of them.

WILL JAMES

17

The Love of a Dog

The love of a dog is bigger than love,
When they lay their head upon your lap,
Or, when they want to play, anticipating
    with their big brown eyes
Or, when they jump in your car, waiting to go.
But at night when they curl up at the foot
    of the bed,
That's when they know you love them, too.

ALLYSON JOUBERT

Old dogs, like old shoes, are
comfortable. They might
be a bit out of shape and
a little worn around the
edges, but they fit well.

BONNIE WILCOX

Dogs have given us
their absolute all. We
are the center of their
universe. We are the focus of
their love and faith and trust.

ROGER CARAS

Every boy who has a
dog should also have
a mother, so the dog
can be fed regularly.

AUTHOR UNKNOWN

21

A dog teaches a boy fidelity, perseverance, and to turn around three times before lying down.

ROBERT BENCHLEY

I would rather see the portrait of a dog that I know, than all the allegorical paintings they can show me in the world.

SAMUEL JOHNSON

When the Man waked up he said, "What is Wild Dog doing here?" And the Woman said, "His name is not Wild Dog any more, but the First Friend, because he will be our friend for always and always and always."

RUDYARD KIPLING
Just So Stories for Little Children

The disposition of noble dogs is to be gentle with people they know and the opposite with those they don't know.... How, then, can the dog be anything other than a lover of learning since it defines what's its own and what's alien.

PLATO

There is no domestic animal which has so radically altered its whole way of living, indeed its whole sphere of interests, that has become domestic in so true a sense as the dog.

Konrad Lorenz

It is just this rage for consideration that has betrayed the dog into his satellite position as the friend of man. The cat, an animal of franker appetites, preserves his independence. But the dog, with one eye ever on the audience, has been wheedled into slavery, and praised and patted into the renunciation of his nature. Once he ceased hunting and became man's plate-licker, the Rubicon was crossed. Thenceforth he was a gentleman of leisure; and except the few whom we keep working, the whole race grew more and more self-conscious, mannered and affected.

Robert Louis Stevenson

I used to look at [my dog] Smokey and think, "If you were a little smarter you could tell me what you were thinking," and he'd look at me like he was saying, "If you were a little smarter, I wouldn't have to."

FRED JUNGCLAUS

Having once been punished, dogs remember, but like children, they hope they won't be caught in the act.

BARBARA WOODHOUSE

One reason a dog can be such a comfort when you're feeling blue is that he doesn't try to find out why.

AUTHOR UNKNOWN

The dog is mentioned in
the Bible eighteen times—
the cat not even once.

W.E. FARBSTEIN

HOME IS WHERE ~~THE~~ dog ~~CAT~~ IS

A dog will make eye contact. A cat will, too, but a cat's eyes don't even look entirely warm-blooded to me, whereas a dog's eyes look human except less guarded. A dog will look at you as if to say, "What do you want me to do for you? I'll do anything for you." Whether a dog can in fact, do anything for you if you don't have sheep (I never have) is another matter. The dog is willing.

ROY BLOUNT

29

Our dogs will love and admire the meanest of us, and feed our colossal vanity with their uncritical homage.

AGNES REPPLIER

To get the full value of a joy you must have somebody to divide it with.

MARK TWAIN

The love dogs give to humans somehow cannot be lost into nothingness. The fact that He created such a beautiful thing as a dog is very obviously part of His pattern and plan for our joy and the joy of humanity.

FATHER JOHN ANDREW

No matter how little
money and how few
possessions you own, having
a dog makes you rich.

LOUIS SABIN